Elyria Public Library
320 Washington Ave.
Elyria, OH 44035
(440) 323-5747

D1200434

JAN 03 2007

ROBOZONES

ROBOT VOYAGERS

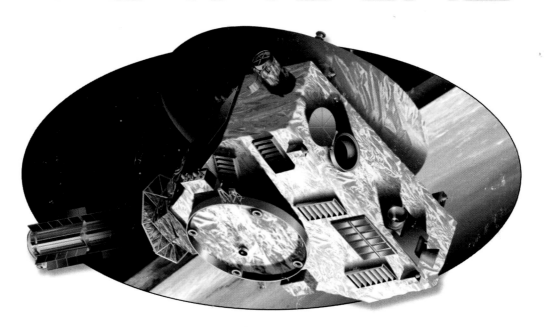

DAVID JEFFERIS

Crabtree Publishing Company
www.crabtreebooks.com

INTRODUCTION

What is a robot? That is a question with no official answer, but robots are usually described as machines that are able to perform tasks on their own or under remote control from a human.

The robots of science fiction books and movies often have a human shape but in the real world, robots come in all shapes and sizes. They all have a computer "brain" which processes information and operates the robot.

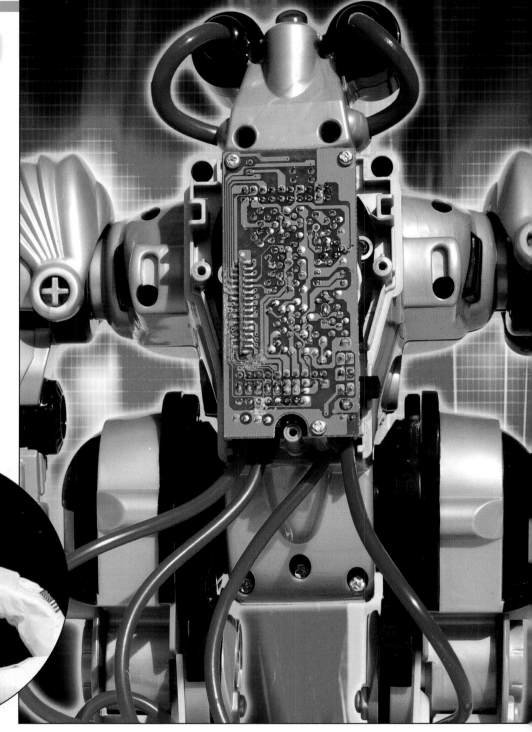

![Crabtree logo] Crabtree Publishing Company
www.crabtreebooks.com

PMB 16A
350 Fifth Ave.
Ste. 3308
New York
NY 10118

616 Welland Ave
St. Catharines, ON
Canada
L2M 5V6 .

Edited by
Isabella McIntyre

Coordinating editor
Ellen Rodger

Project editors
Carrie Gleason

Rachel Eagen
Adrianna Morganelli
L. Michelle Nielsen

Production coordinator
Rose Gowsell

Educational advisor
Julie Stapleton

Technical consultant
Mat Irvine FBIS

Created and produced by
David Jefferis/Buzz Books

©2007 David Jefferis/Buzz Books

**Library and Archives Canada
Cataloguing in Publication**

Jefferis, David
        Robot voyagers / David Jefferis.

(Robozones)
Includes index.
ISBN-13: 978-0-7787-2884-9 (bound)
ISBN-10: 0-7787-2884-6 (bound)
ISBN-13: 978-0-7787-2898-6 (pbk.)
ISBN-10: 0-7787-2898-6 (pbk.)

        1. Mobile robots--Juvenile
literature. I. Title. II. Series.

TJ211.415.J43 2006
j629.8'932   C2006-902861-3

**Library of Congress
Cataloging-in-Publication Data**

Jefferis, David.
    Robot voyagers / written by David
Jefferis.
        p. cm. -- (Robozones)
    Includes index.
    ISBN-13: 978-0-7787-2884-9 (rlb)
    ISBN-10: 0-7787-2884-6 (rlb)
    ISBN-13: 978-0-7787-2898-6 (pbk)
    ISBN-10: 0-7787-2898-6 (pbk)
    1. Mobile robots--Juvenile literature. I.
Title. II. Series: Jefferis,
David. Robozones.
TJ211.415.J44 2006
    629.8'92--dc22
                          2006016041

*All rights reserved. No part of this publication
may be reproduced, stored in a retrieval system
or be transmitted in any form or by any means,
electronic, mechanical, photocopying, recording,
or otherwise, without the prior written permission
of Crabtree Publishing Company.*

Pictures on these pages, clockwise from above left:
1 NASA Robonaut.
2 Complex circuits reveal the position of a robot's computer brain.
3 Future Mars lander robot.
4 Experimental Fujitsu HOAP-1 robot.

Previous page shows:
An illustration of the New Horizons robot probe passing the planet Pluto, planned for 2015.

CONTENTS

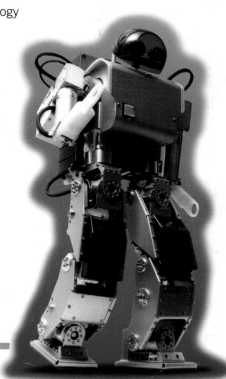

EARLY ROBOT VOYAGERS

Using robots for exploration started in the early years of the space age. In 1957, the world's first artificial satellite was blasted into space.

▲ Shakey was named after its jerky motions. It had bump sensors, a TV camera, and a range-finder to check distances.

The first space robot was the Russian satellite **Sputnik** 1. It was followed by many others, including the Vanguard, launched by the United States in 1959. These space machines were robotic, but they did not look much like our idea of robots. The first robot that could act on its own was Shakey, built in 1966. Shakey was little more than a box on wheels, but it was the first robot that could perform simple tasks, such as moving and turning.

◀ Sputnik 1 (far left) was the first space satellite. The U.S. followed with its Vanguard satellite (left).

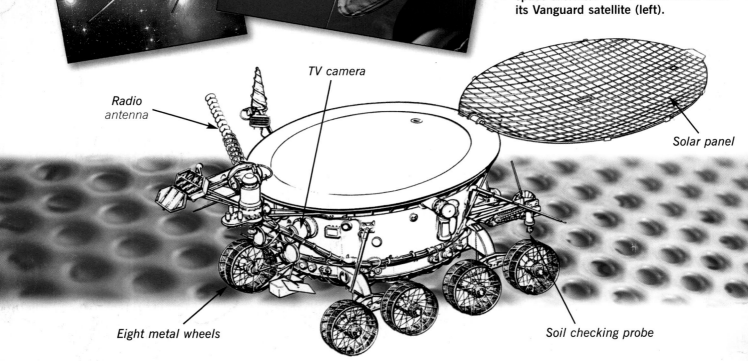

Radio antenna

TV camera

Solar panel

Eight metal wheels

Soil checking probe

▲ Lunokhod was powered by a big solar panel, which changed the Sun's energy to electricity. It covered 6.5 miles (10 kilometers) before being switched off.

The 1960s were the years of the "space race" between Russia and the U.S., with each trying to outdo the other in a race to explore space. In 1970, Russia's Lunokhod became the first robot to drive across the Moon's surface. It worked for nearly a year after landing, testing the Moon's soil, and taking 20,000 TV pictures.

▲ A rover **rolls across the sands of Mars. The picture at top right shows the type of robot that may help astronauts when they return to the Moon in the future.**

Today, robot voyagers have explored much of the **Solar System**, including planets, moons, **comets**, and other space objects. There are still new places to go, such as the distant, icy world of Pluto and, nearer to home, the rust-red deserts of the planet Mars.

ROBOFACTS: METAL HEROES OF SCI-FI

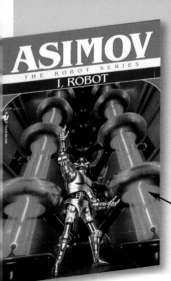

Our ideas of how robots should look and behave have been formed largely from the world of science fiction books and movies.

One of the best-known writers on the subject was Isaac Asimov. Asimov wrote a series of popular robot books. He even determined the three "Laws of Robotics," which defined robotic behavior.

This Asimov robot book was first published in 1950

The most important Law was that a robot should protect humans from harm. Of course there have been many fictional robots that have ignored Asimov's Laws!

An early robot character was Robby, from the 1956 movie *Forbidden Planet*. Robby was played by an actor, in a costume that looked and sounded convincing.

The 7-foot, 2-inch (218-cm) Robby was a helpful character

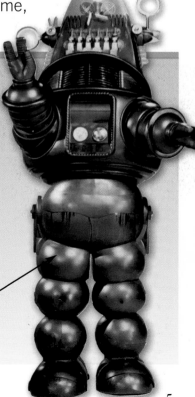

ROBOTS ON THE MOVE

How do robots travel across the ground? Many of them roll on wheels. Others crawl on caterpillar-like tracks, or can walk on metal legs.

▲ Each S-bot has an outer pair of wheels and an inner set of tracks. This system is called "treels."

▲ Five S-bots swarm together to cross uneven terrain. Up to 35 S-bots could work together in a big swarm.

Robots use tracks for better grip while moving over uneven surfaces. S-bots are robots that use both wheels and tracks. They use wheels for flat surfaces and tracks for rough terrain. S-bots were created as part of a Swiss study into how insects work together in swarms. Acting like insects, the S-bots move independently, or group together as a swarm. They swarm when several are needed to do things that one S-bot cannot do alone, such as crossing a gap between rocks.

▲ The Tetwalker moves by flopping along, end over end. Tests show that its pyramid shape makes it steady when crossing rough ground.

▶ These little machines are among the smallest robots made. Each weighs less than one ounce (28 grams), yet can crawl 20 inches (50 centimeters) a minute!

Very small robots, called micro robots, use tracks to crawl inside pipes and other tight spots. The smallest are only 0.5 inches (13 millimeters) long, yet can find their way through an obstacle course without outside help. Each one is powered by two electric motors and three watch batteries.

ROBOFACTS: RESCUE BY ROBODOG?

Researchers at the Georgia Institute of Technology have been experimenting with AIBO robodogs to see if they could be used as something more than just expensive toys.

The researcher in the picture adjusts an AIBO that is ready to walk aboard the red vehicle, an ATRV-Mini robot transporter. This demonstration took place in the BORG laboratory.

The BORG research center was named after the scary cyborgs in the *Star Trek* television series.

The researchers are studying ways to use robots to aid at disaster sites. The demonstration showed how a pair of AIBOs could be taken on a search and rescue mission. Once there, they could jump off, batteries freshly-charged, ready to go looking for survivors.

O ne of the most advanced walking robots is the Sony **AIBO,** a robotic toy dog that was released in 1999. AIBO, named after the computer software that runs it, has been made in several models, including the ERS220, shown here. AIBOs are remarkable. They can learn about their environment, recognize voices and faces, and can be taught new behavior by their owners.

▼ AIBO robots are no longer made, but you can find them for sale on Internet auction sites.

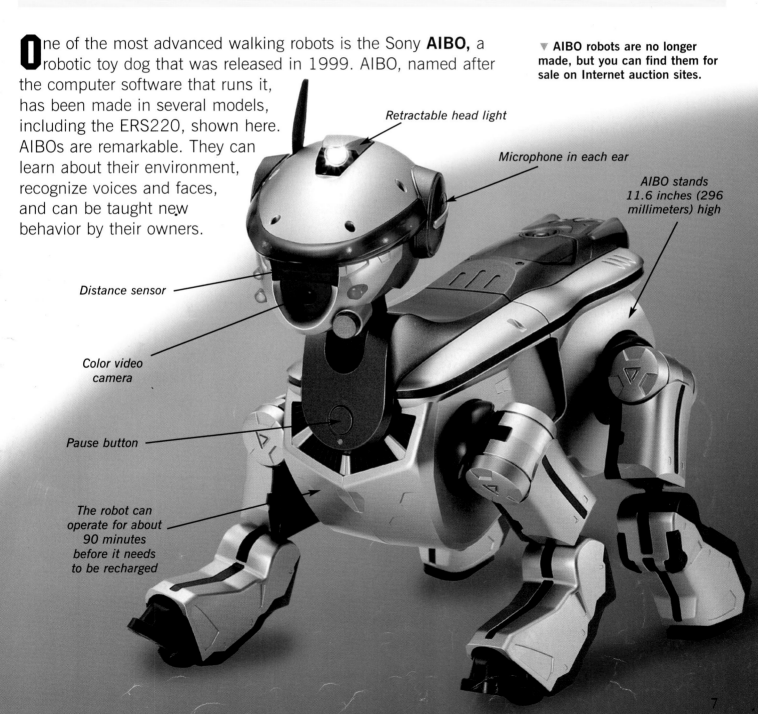

Retractable head light

Microphone in each ear

AIBO stands 11.6 inches (296 millimeters) high

Distance sensor

Color video camera

Pause button

The robot can operate for about 90 minutes before it needs to be recharged

7

ROBOTS IN EXTREME ZONES

Robots can explore places that are too difficult or dangerous for humans to go, including volcanoes, earthquake zones, and areas of temperature extremes.

Volcanoes are dangerous places. Even if there is no eruption, there are often gases that can poison humans. Research robots are used to gather information where humans cannot. The Dante II walking robot was tested inside a volcano in the 1990s. The newer, wheeled Robovolc robot can roll up to a volcano to measure gases and take photographs.

Blue Dragon is a robot that can creep and crawl over awkward terrain. Blue Dragon has three sections that turn, bend, and even roll sideways like the body of a snake. The robot's Japanese builders think that in the future, robots like Blue Dragon could be used over terrain broken up by earthquakes.

▲ Robovolc is a wheeled robot with sensors that provide images (top) showing hot spots inside a volcano.

▼ Blue Dragon was designed to wriggle through earthquake rubble to hunt for trapped survivors using its on-board cameras and heat detectors.

Blue Dragon's Caterpillar treads grip on rough surfaces

A camera inside the front section gives a forward view

▲ Nomad was built to search for meteorites, or rocks that fall from space, in the frozen landscape of Antarctica. It was also tested in the Atacama Desert in Chile.

◄ The Dante II walking robot was used to take readings from a volcano on Mount Spurr in Alaska. It fell sideways while walking out of the volcano, but still gave researchers valuable information.

ROBOFACTS: DISASTER RESCUE

Researchers in the United States are developing robots that can work together in groups, communicating by radio to each other as they track down an object.

In the picture at right, three of these robots are being tested to see if they could find a skier buried in an avalanche. In a real disaster, robots could save lives by finding people before they freeze to death.

The robots in the photo are not looking for an actual body. They are homing in on signals from an emergency radio beacon buried under several feet of snow. Skiers carrying beacons could be tracked down quickly.

A glove shows the position of a radio beacon buried in the snow

UNDERSEA VOYAGERS

▲ A robotic inspection of the wrecked *Titanic*. The ship had sunk to a depth of 12,460 feet (3,798 meters).

Robots are ideal for working in the oceans. Unlike humans, they do not need air, and can be built strong enough to withstand the pressure of deep water.

The deep-diving robotic craft *Jason Junior* made the news in 1986, when it helped explore the wreck of the *Titanic*. The *Titanic* was a passenger ship that sunk in 1919 in the Atlantic Ocean after hitting an iceberg. *Jason Junior* was controlled by scientists aboard a submarine in the water nearby.

◄ The Super Scorpio can dive to 5000 feet (1,524 meters). Its robotic arms can lift heavy debris out of the way.

Deep-sea rescue is the main purpose for the *Super Scorpio* robot. The *Super Scorpio* is controlled by a human working on a ship. Commands are given to the robot through a thick cable. *Super Scorpio* has powerful metal arms with strong grippers. Its job is to help free the crew of a submarine too damaged to return to the surface.

ROBOFACTS:
UNDERWATER GLIDERS

Underwater gliders are Autonomous Underwater Vehicles (AUVs) that set off from the water's surface in a long underwater glide. They use their wing-like fins to make a long, shallow path.

When the glider nears the bottom, an electric motor pumps a buoyancy tank with air, so the glider bobs up to the surface. Then it sets off in a glide again, repeating the glide-and-float process.

It is not a fast way of traveling, but it uses very little power, so an AUV glider can go further and for much longer than a machine with propellers. Underwater gliders are useful for long ocean sampling missions that can last for days, weeks, or even months at a time.

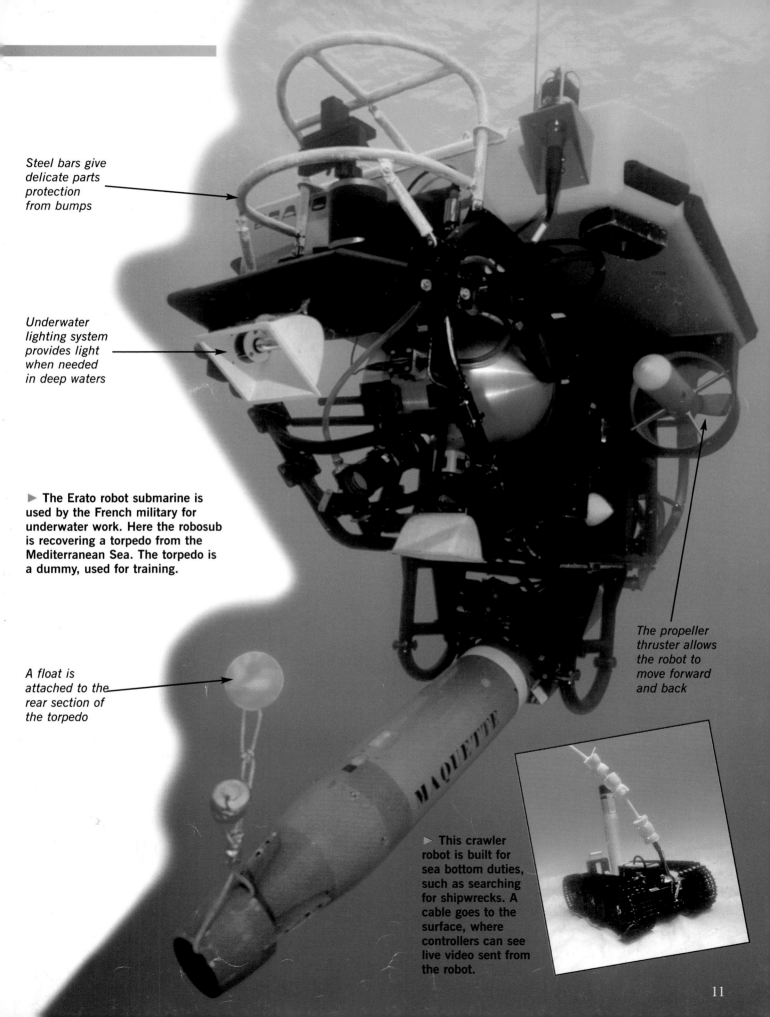

Steel bars give delicate parts protection from bumps

Underwater lighting system provides light when needed in deep waters

▶ The Erato robot submarine is used by the French military for underwater work. Here the robosub is recovering a torpedo from the Mediterranean Sea. The torpedo is a dummy, used for training.

A float is attached to the rear section of the torpedo

The propeller thruster allows the robot to move forward and back

MAQUETTE

▶ This crawler robot is built for sea bottom duties, such as searching for shipwrecks. A cable goes to the surface, where controllers can see live video sent from the robot.

EYES IN THE SKY

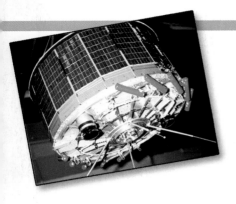

▲ Tiros-1 was the first successful weather satellite. Launched in 1960, the weather robot took TV images of clouds from space. It paved the way for the more advanced robots used today.

Satellites scan the world and take pictures from space. Uncrewed "drones" are aircraft that spy in the sky. Both are robotic machines.

Space satellites are among the most valuable robotic devices. They save both lives and money. For example, satellites can detect forest fires, which might otherwise rage out of control. Satellite images also show the effects of **pollution** all over the planet, helping alert us to the damage humans are doing to the environment.

▼ The uncrewed Coyote sky-spy plane can be launched in mid-air by navy patrol planes or from a ground vehicle. Folding wings enable the Coyote to be carried in a launch tube just 4.5 inches (11.5 centimeters) across.

Camera-equipped robotic aircraft are used as "sky-spies." They are small, easy to use, and do not risk any lives if they are shot down in wars.

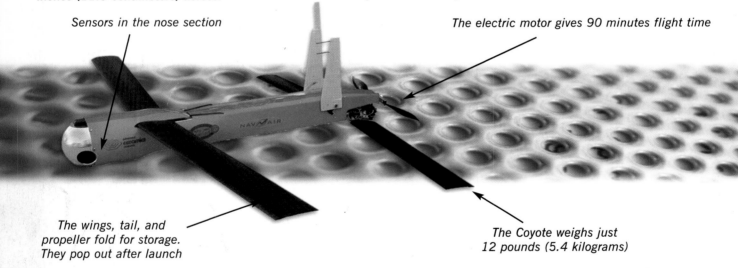

Sensors in the nose section

The electric motor gives 90 minutes flight time

The wings, tail, and propeller fold for storage. They pop out after launch

The Coyote weighs just 12 pounds (5.4 kilograms)

▲ Small robotic aircraft can be carried neatly in a case, then assembled quickly for flight.

▲ Pilots can use a TV-equipped hood and hand controls to fly.

▲ Some small roboplanes can land after a mission by flying into a net.

▲ The camera-equipped Altair UAV is an advanced version of the Predator. Altair can fly for up to 32 hours at a time before needing to land for refueling.

One of the most advanced roboplanes is the Predator **Uncrewed Air Vehicle** (UAV). It can fly by itself using a computer program or be directed from the ground by a pilot using a TV screen and control stick. Pilots say that flying the Predator is like "looking through a straw," because the view from a TV screen is narrower than the view from a real cockpit.

ROBOFACTS:
POLLUTION WATCHDOG

Robotic satellites circling the Earth help check on the health of the planet.

The biggest robotic pollution watcher satellite is called Envisat. At 23 feet (7 meters) long, it is the size of a small truck. Envisat is packed with sensors to study what is going on in the planet's atmosphere and on the surface.

Envisat studies pollution in cities, dusty deserts, and ash belching out of volcanoes.

The satellite is not stopped by clouds or bad weather, because it has radar that passes straight through such obstacles. Envisat passes 500 miles (800 kilometers) above the Earth and can map the entire planet in a few days.

At launch, Envisat weighed more than 8.8 tons (8 tonnes)

An Envisat picture shows haze from industrial pollution in China

13

This robocar, named Tommy, has a main processing computer that costs less than $200.

ROBOT RACERS

New cars already have computers that guide their mechanical systems. Eventually, some vehicles will have robotic systems that take over completely.

The cutting edge of robotic vehicle design is shown off at the annual Grand Challenge race, organized by **DARPA**, a department of the U.S. military. The 2005 Challenge covered 132 miles (212 kilometers) of twisting trails through the Mojave Desert. There were 23 entries, but only five of them completed the course successfully.

▶ One race vehicle, Sandstorm, had a silver dome on top. Inside was a laser beam that scanned ahead and made hairpin bends easier to follow. Sandstorm finished in second place, in a time of just over seven hours.

▼ This entrant was built on the frame of a dune buggy.

Vehicles in the race had various ways of keeping on the dusty course. One vehicle, called Sandstorm, had a **laser** eye that swept a beam of light across the landscape. Sandstorm's computer translated reflections from the beam to a digital map that determined the difference between level ground and sloping areas. Sandstorm then followed the level route.

And the winner is... a robocar called Stanley! Here the team takes the 2005 winner's stand.

▼ Stanley used laser and video equipment to steer. The lasers showed flat and smooth ground. Then a computer system matched their input with video data from the camera. When the two patterns matched, the computer determined the way was clear for Stanley to move ahead. Stanley covered the course in less than seven hours.

Five laser beam scanners

Radio antenna

TV camera

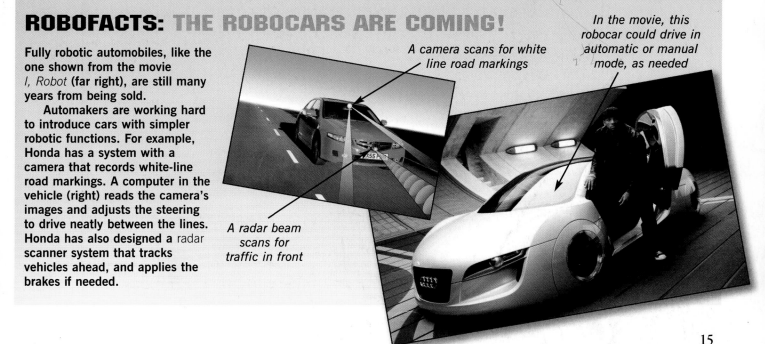

ROBOFACTS: THE ROBOCARS ARE COMING!

Fully robotic automobiles, like the one shown from the movie *I, Robot* (far right), are still many years from being sold.

Automakers are working hard to introduce cars with simpler robotic functions. For example, Honda has a system with a camera that records white-line road markings. A computer in the vehicle (right) reads the camera's images and adjusts the steering to drive neatly between the lines. Honda has also designed a radar scanner system that tracks vehicles ahead, and applies the brakes if needed.

A camera scans for white line road markings

In the movie, this robocar could drive in automatic or manual mode, as needed

A radar beam scans for traffic in front

BIOBOTS

Biorobotics **is the science of making robots move like animals or insects. Some biorobotic machines fly or crawl like insects, while others swim like fish.**

▲ This is one of several flying insect designs. It measures just 0.4 inches (10 millimeters) across.

▲ This eight-legged lobster robot can walk on a beach or as deep as 40 feet (12 meters) under water.

Robolobster is one of the first robots whose design was based on a living animal. Robolobster even has artificial muscles, made of **nitinol**, a material that shrinks and expands like a real muscle. Robolobster was made to search for buried explosives. Its design was based on real lobsters because they use their eight legs to crawl around in muddy water.

▼ Robotuna splits in two, so that it can be serviced.

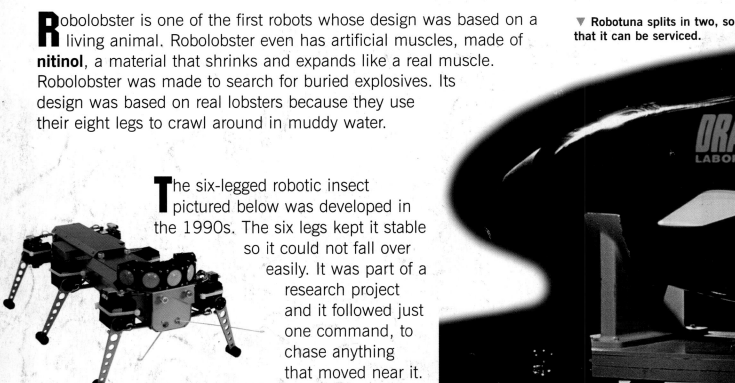

The six-legged robotic insect pictured below was developed in the 1990s. The six legs kept it stable so it could not fall over easily. It was part of a research project and it followed just one command, to chase anything that moved near it.

The International Robot Olympiad Committee (IROC) holds competitive robot sporting events. Robot designers team up to pit their robots against others in events such as boxing, basketball, or soccer. The designers are college and university students who are learning about robotics in school. IROC's many competitions help improve the science of robotics. To win an event, designers have to make robots that are quicker and perform tasks better than the other teams' robots. Every year, entrants get a little better. Competitors learn from the mistakes made by others in the previous year's competition.

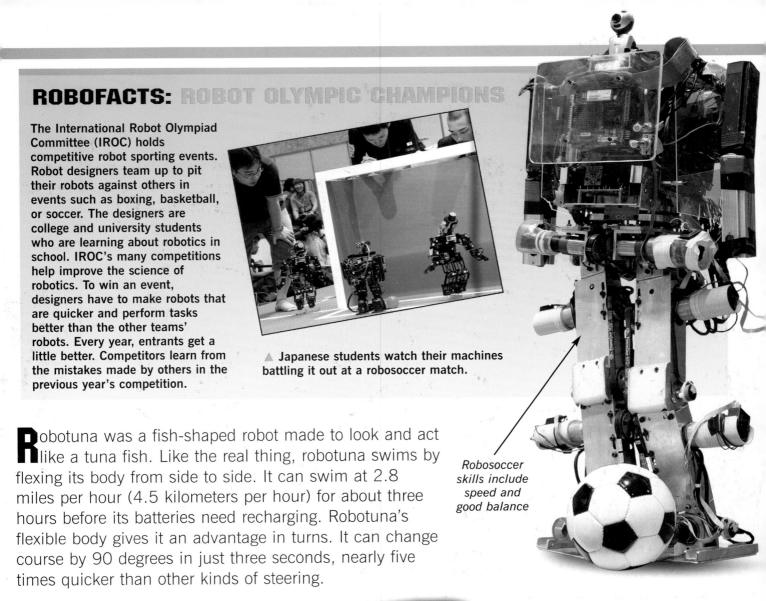

▲ Japanese students watch their machines battling it out at a robosoccer match.

Robosoccer skills include speed and good balance

Robotuna was a fish-shaped robot made to look and act like a tuna fish. Like the real thing, robotuna swims by flexing its body from side to side. It can swim at 2.8 miles per hour (4.5 kilometers per hour) for about three hours before its batteries need recharging. Robotuna's flexible body gives it an advantage in turns. It can change course by 90 degrees in just three seconds, nearly five times quicker than other kinds of steering.

The tail has four movable links, covered by plastic scales. These keep the surface smooth when the tail bends

HANDY ROBOTS

Researchers are developing robots that can help humans work in space, including robots that can grip things as well as a human can.

▲ Shown here being tested in a jet, GYRE (arrowed) is a free-floating robot made for work in space.

Making a robot that can use its hands and arms as well as a human is a tall order. Robonaut is a project being developed by scientists at the space agency NASA. Robonaut's hands were designed to be sensitive, like human hands.

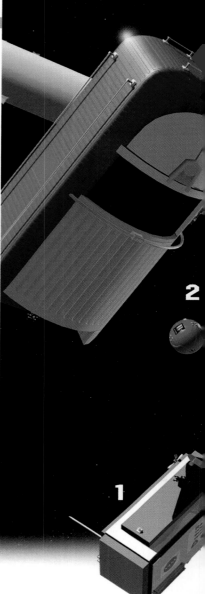

2

1

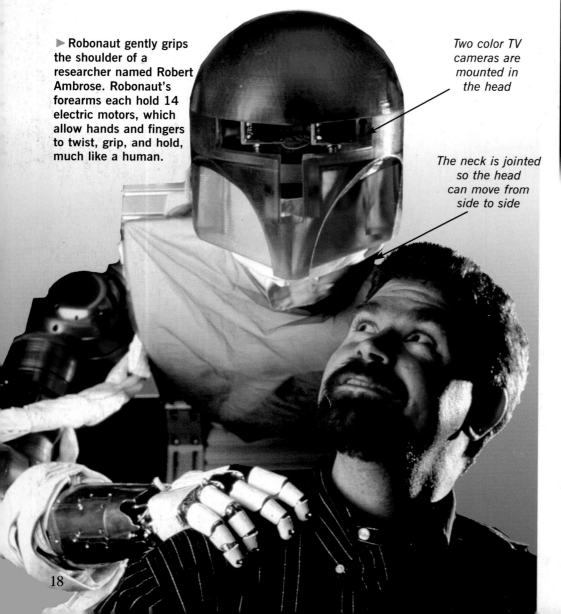

▶ Robonaut gently grips the shoulder of a researcher named Robert Ambrose. Robonaut's forearms each hold 14 electric motors, which allow hands and fingers to twist, grip, and hold, much like a human.

Two color TV cameras are mounted in the head

The neck is jointed so the head can move from side to side

If Robonaut goes into space, a human operator will direct it. The operator will wear goggles to see through Robonaut's TV eyes, and a special suit and gloves that act as a command system for the robot. Any action the operator makes will be sent to the robot by a radio link. This system is called **telepresence**.

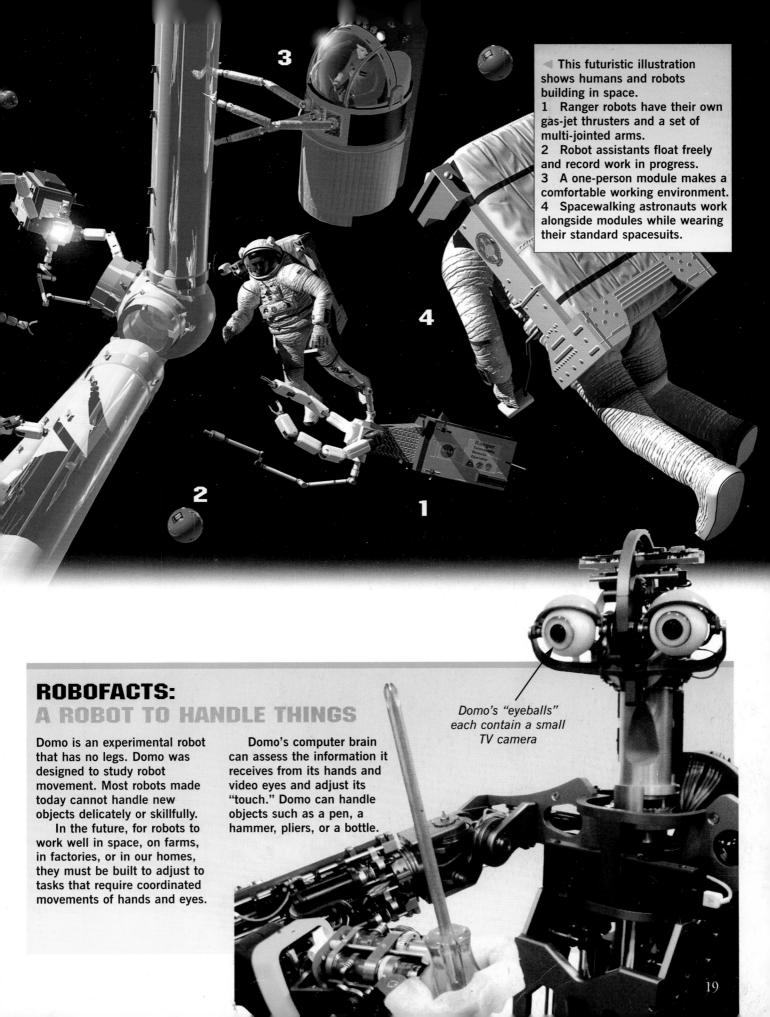

This futuristic illustration shows humans and robots building in space.

1 Ranger robots have their own gas-jet thrusters and a set of multi-jointed arms.

2 Robot assistants float freely and record work in progress.

3 A one-person module makes a comfortable working environment.

4 Spacewalking astronauts work alongside modules while wearing their standard spacesuits.

Domo's "eyeballs" each contain a small TV camera

ROBOFACTS:
A ROBOT TO HANDLE THINGS

Domo is an experimental robot that has no legs. Domo was designed to study robot movement. Most robots made today cannot handle new objects delicately or skillfully.

In the future, for robots to work well in space, on farms, in factories, or in our homes, they must be built to adjust to tasks that require coordinated movements of hands and eyes.

Domo's computer brain can assess the information it receives from its hands and video eyes and adjust its "touch." Domo can handle objects such as a pen, a hammer, pliers, or a bottle.

RED PLANET ROVERS

The planet Mars has been visited by many robot explorers since the 1970s. Today's robots may be small but they carry a wide range of research tools.

Digging arm

▲ The Beagle 2 Mars probe was built to dig deep for soil samples. Beagle's designers thought that living things might survive underground protected from the harsh environment by layers of soil. Sadly, there was no chance to find out, as contact with the probe was lost during landing.

Mars is millions of miles away from Earth. Sending robot probes all the way to Mars is not an easy job. The journey itself takes several months, and conditions on Mars are much harsher than on Earth.

Many robot probes have lost contact with Earth during the long flight and others have failed on landing. The ones that did make it sent back images of a planet with huge volcanoes, deep valleys, and icy poles.

Earth

Mars

◀ Mars is a smaller planet than Earth. It is covered with rust-red deserts and has no oceans or breathable air.

The United States launched the Viking landers in the 1970s. These explorers stayed put once they landed. Since then, wheeled rovers have been sent to Mars. In 1997, the Sojourner rover explored Mars for nearly three months before its power supply failed.

ROBOFACTS:
FIRST ROBOTS ON MARS

In 1976, two U.S. Viking robotic space probes landed on Mars. Each Viking carried a small laboratory to carry out tests on Martian wind and weather, and also to see if there were signs of life on the surface.

Each Viking had a long metal arm, which scooped up a sample of soil. The soil was then checked in the laboratory to see if there was anything living in it.

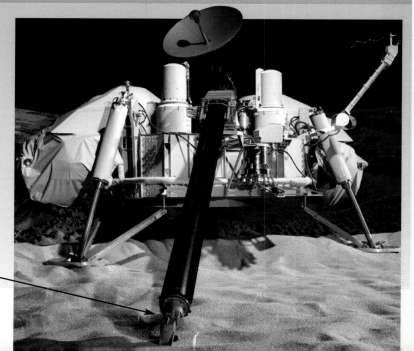

Soil scoop

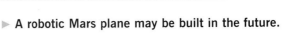

▶ A robotic Mars plane may be built in the future.

▼ Mars rovers have to cope with daytime temperatures no higher than 34°Fahrenheit (10°Celsius) and icy nights that plunge below -13°F (-25°C). During daylight hours, solar panels produce electricity for the electric motors and other equipment.

Antenna

Cameras mounted on top of pole for a good view around the rover

Solar panels generate electricity

Radio and TV antenna

A compartment in the rover's body keeps delicate equipment warm

A set of cameras is also mounted in front of rover

Electric motor in each wheel

Two later Mars rovers, Spirit and Opportunity, landed in 2004. They were each about the size of a small refrigerator, and had six small electric-powered wheels, giving a top speed of about two inches (five centimeters) per second. This may seem slow, but a rover could crash into a large rock if it traveled any faster. The metal wheels had spikes to grip the dusty desert surface.

▲ **Future spiderbots may walk across rugged areas of Mars.**

COMET CATCHERS

Robotic spaceprobes travel great distances to inspect comets and other space debris.

▲ The collector plate was a vital part of the Stardust probe. It was used to scoop up bits of comet dust.

Comets are space objects made of ice, dust, and rock. For much of their existence, comets move far from the Sun's warming rays.

Sometimes a comet passes close to the Sun. The Sun's heat then vaporizes some of the comet's ice, resulting in a long, glowing tail.

The core or nucleus of comet Wild 2 is about three miles (five kilometers) long

Stardust's return capsule is carried back after a safe landing

▲ Stardust passes through the shining tail of comet Wild 2 (pronounced "Vilt 2").

In 2006, the Stardust spaceprobe returned a capsule to Earth, after passing through the tail of comet Wild 2. Inside the capsule were samples of comet dust collected from the tail. Scientists are studying the dust to learn more about comets.

Deep Impact's penetrator probe blew away a large chunk from the comet

ROBOFACTS: BULLSEYE ON A COMET

Another comet encounter was made by the Deep Impact robot explorer in 2005, when it fired a penetrator probe at the comet Tempel 1. The probe hit the comet at a speed of more than 6.2 miles per second (10 km/s), with an impact force of nearly 5.5 tons (five tonnes) of explosives. Deep Impact recorded information about the debris blown off the comet's surface.

The penetrator probe

This picture sequence shows the explosion as the penetrator hits Tempel 1

Deep Impact's instruments recorded events from a safe distance

Tempel 1 rotates once every 41 hours. It approaches the Sun every five and a half years

23

VOYAGES TO INFINITY

Robot voyagers have traveled far beyond Mars. They have been sent to other planets, circling in the cold, outer reaches of the Solar System.

◀ A protective capsule (1) contained the Huygens probe (2).

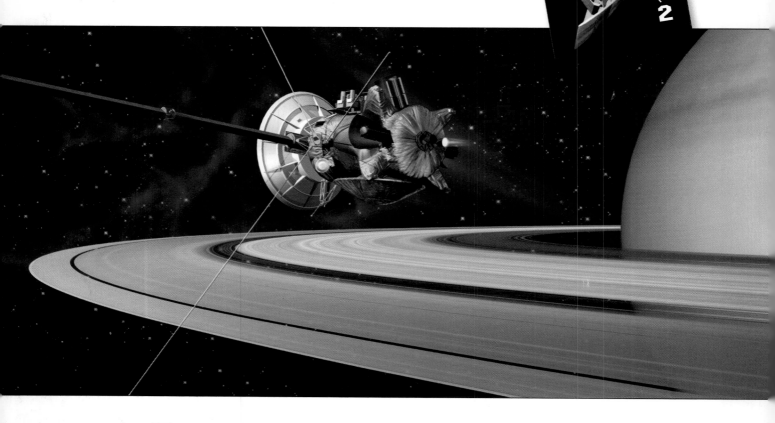

▼ The Russian Progress was the first robotic space cargo ship. It is used to resupply the International Space Station.

The ringed planet Saturn is a giant. It measures 75,000 miles (120,000 kilometers) across, or nearly ten times the width of Earth. Saturn has almost 50 moons, the largest of which is called Titan.

Titan is the only moon in the Solar System with a dense atmosphere. This has made it a fascinating area of study for a spaceprobe called Cassini.

▲ The Cassini robot probe went into orbit around Saturn by firing its braking rocket after the long trip from Earth. Here it is flying above Saturn's rings, made of icy particles ranging in size from boulders to dust grains.

Cassini carried a smaller probe, called **Huygens**. It was aimed at Titan in January 2005, more than seven years after the mission blasted off from Earth. Huygens parachuted through the smoggy atmosphere and landed on a surface that was crunchy on top and softer underneath. Scientists think this surface is made up of a super-cold mud.

▼ The Huygens probe sets off on its mission to Titan. Titan's hazy air layers keep the surface hidden.

► Huygens used parachutes to land gently on Titan. The picture below right is based on photos taken by the probe. The pebbles are about the size of a human hand and are made of ice. Titan is a very cold world, with a surface temperature of about -192°Fahrenheit (-180°Celsius).

ROBOFACTS:
FIRST TRIP TO PLUTO

Only the planet Pluto has not been visited by robot voyagers. Pluto is a distant planet, from where the Sun appears as little more than a bright star. It is too far away from the Sun to receive much light or heat. Even a hot summer's day on Pluto is a chilly -365° Fahrenheit (-220°Celsius). It is a small planet, so small that some scientists say it should not be called a planet at all!

The New Horizons robotic probe was launched in January 2006, and if all goes well, it will fly by Pluto and its moons in 2015. After that, New Horizons will travel on to inspect icy objects even further away from the Sun.

New Horizons will take only a few hours to fly past Pluto

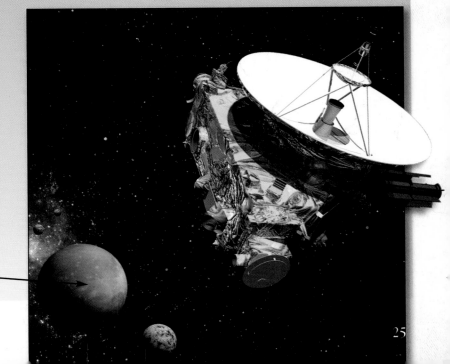

THINGS TO COME?

In the future, robot voyagers will be able to perform many more functions than the machines of today.

The science of robotics has come a long way in the last 50 years. Better and faster computers have given robots the ability to quickly and reliably handle tasks such as manufacturing products or spying on enemies. Scientists have not yet developed robots that can think like humans. Even so, continuing advances in robot research and technology will mean that robots may become a very important part of our daily lives in years to come.

▲ A robonaut as it might look if developed for work in space.

ROBOFACTS: ROBOTS REPLACING HUMANS?

Robot voyagers have already replaced humans for many exploration jobs. A century ago, humans discovered unknown lands – now we send the robots first.

Two big factors will help make future robots better than those of today. Better microchips are the core improvement, because faster processing allows a robot's systems to work more efficiently.

A portable power supply is also vital, as robots need electricity. New battery designs will allow robots to work away from a power socket for long periods, and to recharge their batteries in minutes.

◄ This design for a future robot has several key features, including a very lightweight body, and video eyes that see at night as well as by day.

▲ A swarm of robot probes explore space. These robots are searching for minerals in space rocks.

► These Dragonfly roboplanes could fly and carry cargo without a human pilot.

In space, robots will continue to lead the way. Robot probes like the ones above could drift in space for many years, on survey or exploration missions. The big difference between these probes and the robots of today is that the future probes will have enough computer power to make almost all decisions during a mission. Back on Earth, robot planes, like the ones pictured below, are just one of many kinds of robots that will be in use over the next few years.

Lift fans allow the Dragonfly to take off and land vertically, like a helicopter

TIME TRACK

Here are some of the events and machines in the story of robot voyagers on Earth and across the universe.

▲ A robocar from the 2004 movie, *I, Robot*.

▲ This robot starred in the play *RUR* (Rossum's Universal Robots), by Karel Capek. The word robot means "work" in the Czech language.

▲ Robo One was a star at the 2004 Robolympics. These were held in San Francisco, California.

1920 The Czech writer Karel Capek (1890-1938) creates *RUR*, a play starring robots that tried to take over the world. This is the first known use of the word robot, which was used by Capek's brother, Josef.

1950 Isaac Asimov (1920-1992) writes *I, Robot*, the best-known of a series of novels that focus on robots in the future. Asimov also determined the Laws of Robotics for an earlier story, *Runaround*, from 1942. They state:
1 A robot may not harm a human being, or, through inaction, allow a human being to come to harm.
2 A robot must obey the orders given to it by human beings, except where such orders would conflict with the First Law.
3 A robot must protect its own existence, as long as such protection does not conflict with the First or Second Law.

1956 Robby the robot stars in the movie *Forbidden Planet*.

1957 The first space satellite is launched by Russia. Sputnik 1 weighs 184.3 pounds (83.6 kilograms). In 1958, the first U.S. satellite, Vanguard 1, is launched.

1960 The first successful weather satellite, Tiros-1, sends TV weather pictures back to Earth for 78 days.

1966 Shakey is the first robot that can solve problems, such as moving blocks or past objects in its path. Shakey is now on display at the Computer History Museum, in California.

1968 The first computer circuit on a tiny chip of silicon is perfected. The microchip becomes the basis of all computing machines made since, including robots.

1970 Lunokhod 1 is the first Moon rover, carrying out photography and soil tests for 11 months. American astronauts Neil Armstrong and Buzz Aldrin became the first humans on the Moon the year before, in July 1969. In 1973, another Lunokhod lands, and explores for about four months.

1976 Viking landers touch down on Mars, taking photographs and testing the soil for signs of life.

1978 First flight of the Russian Progress space freighter. Improved models are still made today.

1986 The *Jason Junior* robotic underwater vehicle makes a close inspection of the *Titanic*, which sank in 1919.

1989 Oceanographer Henry Stommel from the U.S. proposes the idea of an underwater glider, which is later used to make robosubs.

1989 First appearance of the dreaded Borg in the science fiction series *Star Trek*. They are cyborgs, or beings that are a mixture of biological and mechanical systems.

1994 The walking Dante II robot is sent inside the crater of Mount Spurr, a volcano in Alaska.

1997 The Nomad robot is sent on a mission to hunt for meteorites in Antarctica. It has gone on various other expeditions since.

1997 The small Sojourner rover lands on Mars, the first mobile robot to do so. For 83 days, the microwave-sized machine sends back information about conditions on Mars.

1998 The International Robot Olympics Committee (IROC) is formed, to promote robotic sports. The first events are held in Korea, in 1999.

1999 The first AIBO entertainment robot is released as a toy. The AIBO and other machines are popular with robotics researchers for experiments.

2002 The Envisat Earth observation satellite is launched. It is the biggest satellite of its kind sent into space, and is designed to measure the environmental health of our planet.

2003 The Beagle 2 robot nearly makes it to Mars, but disappears before landing. It was named after the the first *Beagle*, a ship used by the 19th century naturalist, Charles Darwin, during his research.

2004 The year of the first DARPA Grand Challenge rally for robot vehicles. No vehicles finish this competition, but a robocar called Stanley successfully covers the desert course the following year.

2005 Robot voyagers make news when the Deep Impact robot craft fires a probe at a comet. Also in 2005, the Huygens probe lands on Titan, a moon of the planet Saturn.

2006 Sony stops making and developing AIBO and other robots.

2006 The Stardust probe brings back samples from a comet and the New Horizons probe leaves for the distant planet, Pluto.

2015 As planned, the New Horizons robot probe will fly by Pluto, sending back pictures as it does so.

▲ (top) Engineers work on a rover in a simulated Mars environment. (above) The Deep Impact Earth-return capsule is prepared for flight. The probe was launched in January 2005.

▼ The AIBO ERS7 not only looks cute, but it is useful too. The features of this 2003 robot include a "house sitter" mode, in which it can record movement with its video eyes, then send the images via email!

> ► The microchip (arrowed) is the tiny brain of all robotic devices. This one is smaller than a fingernail.

GLOSSARY

Here are explanations of many technical terms in this book.

AIBO Educational robots made by the Japanese Sony company. The name AIBO stands for Artificial Intelligence RoBOt.

Antenna Any system for sending or receiving radio and TV signals. Antennas come in many shapes and sizes, including rods, cones, and dishes.

Atmosphere The gases that surround a planet. Earth's atmosphere is made mostly of the gases nitrogen and oxygen. One of Saturn's moons, Titan, is the only known moon that has a thick atmosphere. It consists mainly of nitrogen.

Autonomous Underwater Vehicle (AUV) A robotic submarine.

Biorobotics Also known as biomimetics, the word describes systems or machines that mimic those in nature, such as a robot fly with wings like a real insect, or a robot fish that moves by wriggling its tail from side to side.

Comet A moving object in space, made of a mixture of ice, rock, and dust.

Cyborg A combination of both a living creature and a machine.

DARPA Short for Defense Advanced Research Projects Agency. DARPA is a department of the U.S. military that is interested in many advanced technologies, including robotics.

Huygens The Titan lander probe, named after Dutch physicist, mathematician, and astronomer, Christiaan Huygens (1629-1695), who discovered Titan in 1655.

Laser A machine that shines an intense pencil-thin beam of light. A laser beam usually consists of just one color and does not spread out as quickly as ordinary light. A laser can be used to check distances by timing the return of reflected laser energy.

Microchip The tiny, calculating part of any computer or robotic device. The wires and cables of old-fashioned electronics have been greatly reduced by microchips.

Nitinol A type of metal called "memory metal" that goes back to its original shape and size after being bent or stretched, like a piece of elastic. Nitinol can be made from mixtures of various materials. A common blend consists of the metals nickel and titanium.

Pollution Waste and harmful substances that damage our planet's environment. Dirty fumes from industrial smokestacks and vehicle exhaust gases are just two causes of pollution.

Radar An electronic system that sends out a radio beam. Some of the beam may bounce off an object in its path, and be reflected back to the transmitter. This bounce-back is shown as a return or "blip" on a TV screen. Radar beams can pass through clouds, so they can be used to map the surface of places such as one of Saturn's moons, Titan.

Rover A robotic probe that moves around on another planet or moon. So far, such probes have had wheels. Future designs may have wings or legs.

Satellite An object that circles, or orbits, a larger object in space. Satellites may be natural, such as Earth's Moon or Saturn's Titan. In 1957, Sputnik 1 was the world's first artificial, or human-made, satellite. Since then, about 4,000 other satellites have been launched into space.

Sensor The general term for any mechanical device that performs a function similar to, or often better than, human senses. Examples of robotic sensors include cameras and microphones.

Solar panel A flat piece of material that converts the energy in sunlight to electricity. Satellites launched from Earth often use solar panels for power, as do robotic rovers that wander around the desert planet Mars.

Solar System The Sun, and the group of nine planets and their moons that circle it. There are also many other, smaller objects, such as comets and rocky asteroids in the Solar System.

Sputnik The name that Russian scientists gave to some of their early spaceprobes. Sputnik means "little star" in Russian.

Telepresence A system that allows humans to operate a distant robotic device. The human usually looks through a TV screen or goggles, seeing images received from the robot's cameras. The operater works the robot with equipment such as a control-stick and switches, or gloves with built-in sensors. Telepresence gives the human a safe working environment when the robot is in a dangerous place, such as deep water.

▲ **The Nomad rover was built to search for meteorites or chunks of space rock that have fallen to Earth.**

Uncrewed Air Vehicle (UAV) An aircraft that can fly without a human onboard.

ROBOZONES: NEXT STEPS

If you would like to explore the science of robotics further, there are several ways to get involved. The quickest way to get started is with one of the many ready-built robots available.

One of the best of these is the Robosapien robot. This two-foot (60-centimeter) programmable machine has functions such as object recognition, stereo sound detection, and laser tracking.

Robosapien even includes a radar system.

If you enjoy making things, Lego Mindstorms could be for you. This is a system that lets you build a variety of robots. You can add a remote control and various sensors, all run by a central microchip.

There are also many robot kits that let you construct robots such as robosubs or roboinsects that can roam around the home.

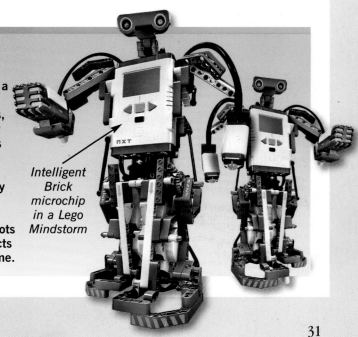

Intelligent Brick microchip in a Lego Mindstorm

INDEX

Acknowledgements
We wish to thank all those individuals and organizations that have helped to create this publication. Information and images were supplied by:
Beagle 2, Brooklyn College/City University of New York, Linda Bucklin, Carnegie Mellon University, DARPA, Aaron Edsinger/ MIT, EDTP Electronics, EPFL/Lausanne, ESA European Space Agency, Fujitsu Corp, General Atomics Corp, Georgia Institute of Technology, GYRE team/ University of Washington, Honda Motor Corp., IROC, IST Information Society Technologies, IS Robotics, iStockphoto, David Jefferis, Evgeny Kuklev, Laboratory of Intelligent Systems/EPFL, Lego, Peter Menzel, NASA Space Agency, Robovolc consortium, Alexis Rosenfeld, Sandia National Laboratories, Science Photo Library, Sony Corp, Lee Stranahan, Toyota Motor Corp, Tokyo Institute of Technology, Trek Aerospace, University of Sherbrooke, US Navy, VAG Auto Group, Webb Research Corp

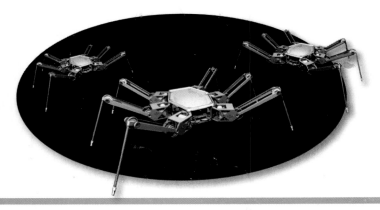

Printed in the U.S.A.